MEMORIES OF CHANGE

It's the Queen's birthday, and the children must work together to create the most amazing machine – a machine that can create 100 apple crumbles by the afternoon tea party.

With growing concerns around mental health, and in the wake of a period of uncertainty and change, it is more important than ever to pay attention to how young children express their emotions, and to teach them to articulate their thoughts in a healthy way. This beautifully illustrated picture book helps children understand the 'journey' in thinking, exploring the ways in which collaborating, experimenting and changing ideas can open new possibilities. By learning to reframe their memories, children learn that change and transition don't have to be bad things.

When it comes to child and adolescent mental health issues, prevention and early intervention are key. The 'serve and return' format of this book provides a virtual space where children can explore thoughts and feelings, teaching them to be resilient in the face of change.

Louise Jackson is a teacher, trainer and author who draws on her direct experience of working with children in schools to develop educational materials that are designed to promote participation, relationships and conversation. She has worked on 'closing the gap' projects with national charities, local authorities, schools, children's centres and training organisations to address educational disadvantage, finding new ways to build capacity and resilience across early childhood services and local communities.

Privileged to have worked alongside many inspirational teachers, practitioners and volunteers in educational settings where vulnerable children are thriving, Louise seeks to capture in her research and writing what it is that makes the difference for young children. Working in collaboration with illustrator Katie Waller, she has created a series of books and practical tools which will help local communities, parents, practitioners and teachers understand the valuable role they can all play in cultivating resilience in early childhood.

A practical guide for early years practitioners
and four children's picture books to
use with 4–6-year-olds.

MEMORIES OF CHANGE

A Thought Bubbles Picture Book About Thinking Differently

Louise Jackson
Illustrated by Katie Waller

Routledge
Taylor & Francis Group

LONDON AND NEW YORK

Cover image credit: Katie Waller

First published 2022
by Routledge
2 Park Square, Milton Park, Abingdon, Oxon OX14 4RN

and by Routledge
605 Third Avenue, New York, NY 10158

Routledge is an imprint of the Taylor & Francis Group, an informa business

British Library Cataloguing-in-Publication Data
A catalogue record for this book is available from the British Library

Library of Congress Cataloging-in-Publication Data
Names: Jackson, Louise, 1964- author. | Waller, Katie, illustrator.
Title: Memories of change : a Thought Bubbles Picture Book about thinking
differently / Louise Jackson ; illustrated by Katie Waller.
Description: First Edition. | New York : Routledge, 2022.
Identifiers: LCCN 2021028618 (print) | LCCN 2021028619 (ebook) | ISBN
9781032135908 (Paperback) | ISBN 9781003230014 (eBook)
Subjects: LCSH: Critical thinking in children. | Cognition in children. |
Group work in education.
Classification: LCC LB1590.3 .J33 2022 (print) | LCC LB1590.3 (ebook) |
DDC 370.15/2--dc23/eng/20211018
LC record available at https://lccn.loc.gov/2021028618
LC ebook record available at https://lccn.loc.gov/2021028619

ISBN: 978-1-032-13590-8 (pbk)
ISBN: 978-1-003-23001-4 (ebk)

DOI: 10.4324/9781003230014

Typeset in Madeleina Sans
by Deanta Global Publishing Services, Chennai, India

It was a lovely sunny autumn day
and all the children were outside
in the exploration garden.

They were sitting, climbing, swinging,
resting and running around the big, old tree.

Along came Queen Ratheena
dressed up for a party.

'Hmm I wonder ...'

said a voice from behind the tree.

'I wonder what we can have to eat
at the birthday tea?'

Pizza?

Porridge?

Pancakes?

Sandwiches?

CAKE?

'Hmm ...
I wonder ...'

What
do you think?

'Something hot ... And crumbly ... Something fruity ... I know!'
said the Queen, hitching up her long dress
and straightening her pearl necklace.

'I want ... I need ... Apple Crumble for my birthday tea!'

The Queen didn't want just **one** apple crumble, not **two** nor even **three**!

Muddley Primary School

The pleasure of your company is requested by

Her Royal Highness The Queen

at a Tea Party in honour of her birthday.

Today at 3 o'clock

Please bring 100 Apple Crumbles.

Can you see
how many?

This was no ordinary request, and the children set to work to create the most amazing machine – a machine that could create 100 apple crumbles by the afternoon tea party.

They **cut**.
　　They **stuck**.
They **drew**.
　　They **painted**.

As the apple crumble machine began to take shape.

Time for a break,
for tea and toast!

Sit down together,
we need to talk.

CAFE

So many plans, so many ideas! Let's stop a while and see where we're at.

This apple crumble machine ...
it's small,
it's big,
it's got chutes,
it's got wheels, a cog and a rig.

It's powered by electricity, with a handle that turns.
A starting button to press and a flashing light.
A shiny mixing bowl with a spinner that churns.

WAIT!

We need to stop –
we need to slow down,
and we need to agree.

If we plan it
together then
maybe just maybe
this will work!

An amazing machine
from one design,
all our ideas in
a single plan.

The hours went by,
as the children worked.
Banging and crashing.
Fixing and joining.

Eventually the machine
began to take shape.

Multiple bits, a few pipes
and some tape.

Together, they returned to the one design,
the single plan.

There was no time to lose, no need to wait.
Joining the parts to make the machine start.

At a quarter to three, the machine was ready.

The Queen left the palace, her visitors were ready.

The countdown began ...

Get ready, set .... Go!

The flashing red button
turned on and ...

The apple crumble machine
SHOOK, **whizzed**
and *whirred*
into life.

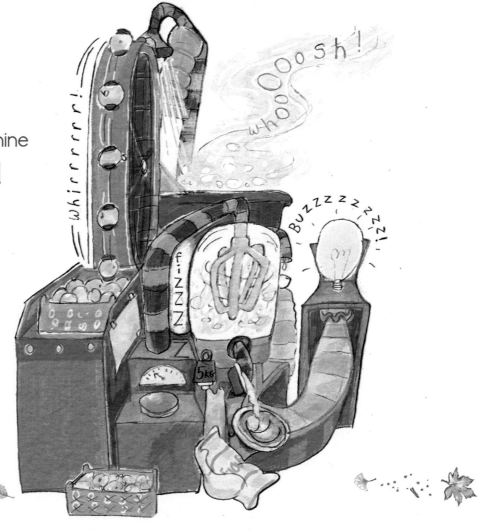

Washing, chopping, crushing and mixing.

Squeezing, squelching, squashing and stirring.

One ... by ... one

the crumbles dropped out of the machine,
steaming hot and ready to eat.

100 puddings, just right for the Queen.

'Oh ... these are delicious!'
'Just perfect for my guests'.

'You're all invited to take a spoonful and test!'

What do you think? These are the best!

So, take another look at the machine and the plan.

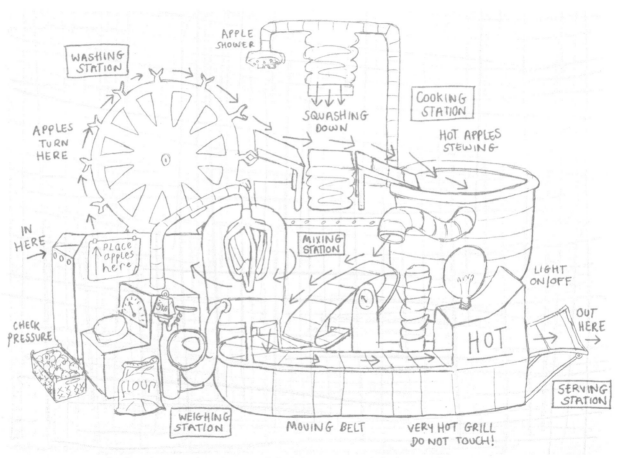

What made it work? How could it run?

If you'd made it yourself, what would you create?
Would you work with others or design on your own?

Would you share your ideas?
Would you get some help?

What do
you think?

What
would
YOU
create?

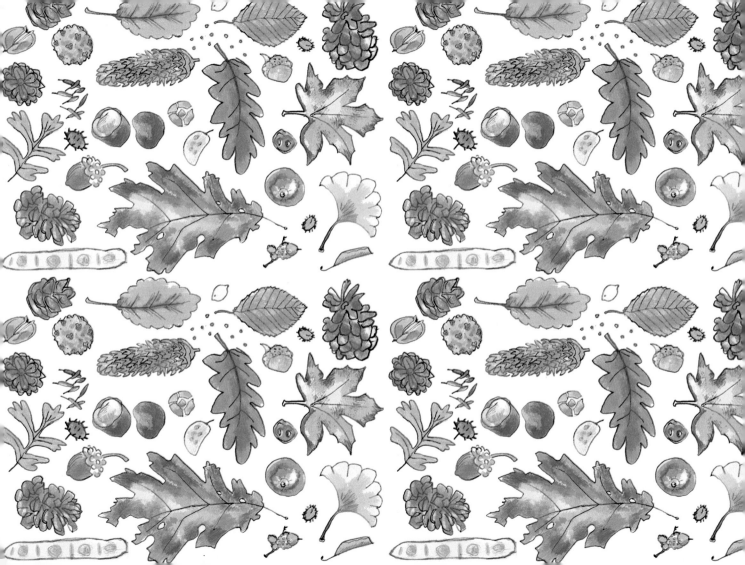